RAYMOND BRIGGS

Ethel & Ernest

PANTHEON BOOKS

NEW YORK

For my Mother & Father

Copyright © 1998 by Raymond Briggs

All rights reserved under International and Pan-American
Copyright Conventions. Published in the United States by Pantheon Books,
a division of Random House, Inc., New York. Originally published in
hardcover in Great Britain in 1998 by Jonathan Cape, London,
and subsequently in the United States in hardcover by Alfred A. Knopf,
a division of Random House, Inc., New York, in 1999.

Pantheon Books and colophon are registered trademarks of
Random House, Inc.

Library of Congress Cataloging-in-Publication Data

Briggs, Raymond.
Ethel & Ernest : a true story / Raymond Briggs.
p. cm.
Originally published: London : Jonathan Cape, 1998.
ISBN 0-375-71447-2
1. Briggs, Ethel, 1895-1971—Comic books, strips, etc. 2. Briggs, Ernest,
1900-1971—Comic books, strips, etc. 3. Great Britain—Biography. I. Title:
Ethel and Ernest. II. Title.
CT788.B7742 B75 2001   941.082'0922—dc21   [B]   2001021578

www.pantheonbooks.com
Printed in Singapore
First American Paperback Edition
2 4 6 8 9 7 5 3 1

Ethel & Ernest

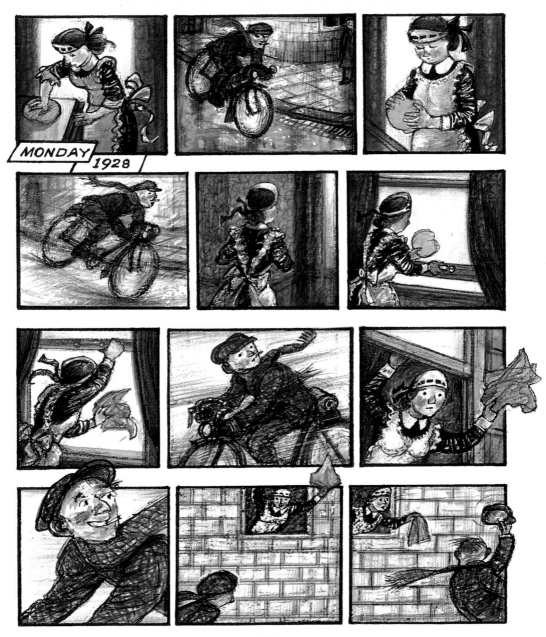

MONDAY 1928

3

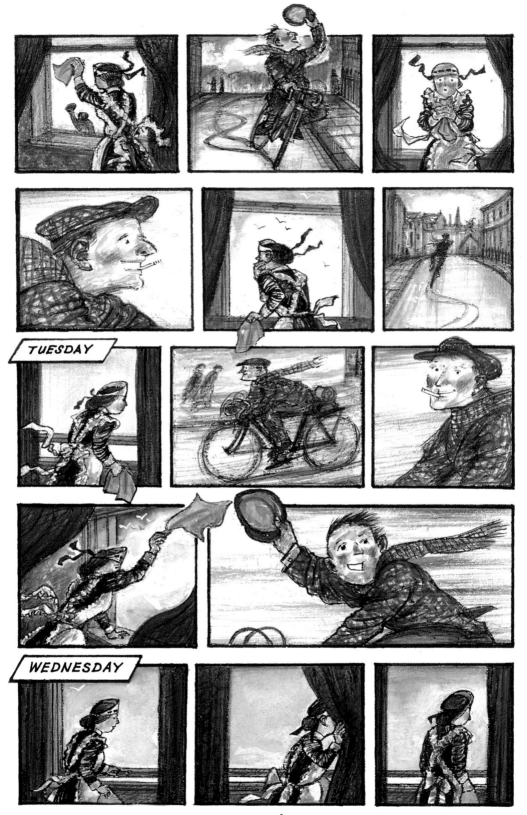

TUESDAY

WEDNESDAY

4

You haven't asked me to **YOUR** home, yet, dear.

Yeah, well... It's not as nice as yours, darling.

Our street's full of diddicois and costermongers. Horses and carts all down the road... Fruit and veg all over the place... Scrap iron, rag and bone men... There's three pubs... Blokes playing cards on the pavement... and there's horse – er... horse manure everywhere. There's fights outside the pubs – women, too ... The coppers won't go down there. The last one that did go, they bashed him up then sat on him and blew his whistle to fetch more coppers. It's not **YOUR** cup of tea, darling.

Oh, Ernest, dear.

Am I to understand that you wish to **LEAVE** us... to get **MARRIED** – to a **MAN** ?

Yes, Madam. Eversosorry, Madam.

1930
~
1940

A wrought-iron gate, your ladyship.

And look, Ernest, a marble pillar!

Oooh! A **FRENCH** window!

We could get those electric lights put in.

Brother Fred's got a wireless. He can hear **GERMANY!**

Ooh! Ernest! Look! There's a **BATHROOM!**

BLIMEY!

The Lovers' Seat

Fairlight Glen   Hastings   1930

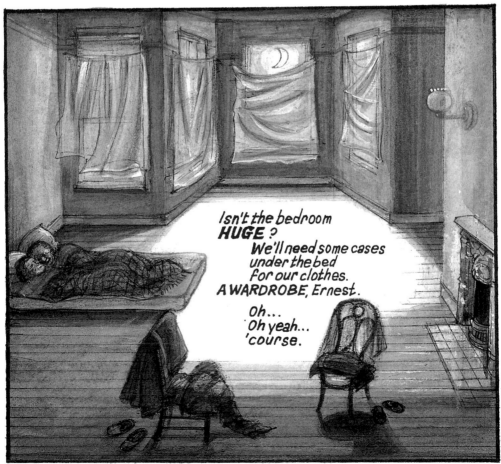

UGH! I hate coal under the stairs! Coal dust gets everywhere and—

It's SO **COMMON!** I'll build a brick bunker in the garden...

That'll be lovely.

Smashing bed! Nearly new. Mahogany, I think... Good springs, look!

Newly-weds need good springs!

Come and try it out, darling...

Certainly **NOT**, Ernest! It's broad **DAYLIGHT!**

17

19

When was it? Hour ago. About five...

I was just doing Ashen Grove.
I nearly run out of Sterilised.
How do you feel?
You look done in. Tired...

It's all red. He...
It's a he...

Mr. Briggs, a word?

It was touch and go.

Oh?

Your wife is thirty-eight.

There had better not be any more.

More children... no more wife.

I'm sorry.

Good day to you.

But we wanted a proper family...

24

29

Whatever are you home for?
You're supposed to be AT SCHOOL!
You mustn't come home in the MIDDLE OF THE DAY!
Did you cross that main road you must have done!

I can't find the
sit down lavatories.
We SHOWED you them!
No. They're GIRLS.
Girls sit down.
NO! There's BOYS' sitting downs as well.

No there ISN'T!
It's all GIRLS.
Look out!
I want to go Number Twos.

Sounds like that Hitler's on the warpath good and proper.

Our George was killed in the last one.

And brother Tom.

It doesn't seem all that long ago.

Our poor old mother never got over it. She died at 48.

Mum!
What have I got to wear
red, white and blue
to school for?
Because it's Empire Day.
What's empire?

Do keep STILL!

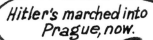

Hitler's marched into Prague, now.

He'll be coming down our road soon.

Adolf Hitler in Wimbledon Park!

It's going to be very stuffy with all this blackout up, Ernest.

Not half as stuffy as a gas-proof room would be.
You have to bung up the chimney, tape over the cracks round doors and windows, put wet newspapers in between the floorboards...

It's a right old barney.

POISON GAS!

I hadn't thought of that.

♪ Underneath the spreading chestnut tree,
Mr. Chamberlain said to me, ♫
if you want your gas mask fitted free —
Join the blinking A.R.P. ♪

33

Russia's invaded Finland now.   I thought they'd invaded POLAND?

Yes, they have.   But you said GERMANY's invaded Poland?

Yes, that's right.   Well, who was it invaded Czechoslovakia?

Germany.   Germany's always invading someone.
I expect they'll invade Russia one day –

Cor blimey! Not likely!
They're IN LEAGUE!   or Russia will invade Germany.

Oh don't be DAFT!   If they ALL keep invading one another,
WE'LL end up invading someone.

Oh Et! You just don't
understand politics.

1940
~
1950

The battle for France is over...
the Battle of Britain is about to begin.
Upon this battle depends the survival
of Christian civilization.
The whole fury and might of the enemy
must, very soon, be turned on us.
Hitler knows that he will have to break us
in this island, or lose the war.

If we can stand up to him, all Europe
may be free and the life of the world
may move forward into broad sunlit uplands.

But, if we fail, the whole world
will sink into the abyss of a new dark age.
Let us, therefore, brace ourselves to our duty
and so bear ourselves that if the
British Empire last for a thousand years,
men will still say:

THIS was their finest hour.

Broad sunlit uplands!

Good old Winston! Our finest hour!

I expect Jerry will be coming over soon.

They're starting to take away our nice gate and railings.

I'll make a wooden gate.

Shame.

They want saucepans, too. They make them into Spitfires.

Funny to think of our front gate being a Spitfire.

44

47

49

Here!
The Court of Appeal has ruled that savings from housekeeping money BELONG TO THE HUSBAND.

YOU don't save from the housekeeping money, do you, dear?

No, never. Only to buy your birthday present.

See? Told you. We've signed a pact with old Joe Stalin. "TWENTY YEAR PACT THROUGH WAR AND PEACE."

It's TWENTY YEARS!

Er... well... I dunno...

Cor! Look! "Women's Fashions–" "SHORTER SKIRTS–" "Bare legs for Patriotism," it says –

Very nice. As long as it lasts.

And how many years was his pact with Hitler?

ERNEST!

Dearest! I've been PROMOTED! I am now a CLERK! CLERK GRADE B3!

No more packing parcels in that rotten, freezing warehouse?

NO! I'm going to work in an OFFICE!

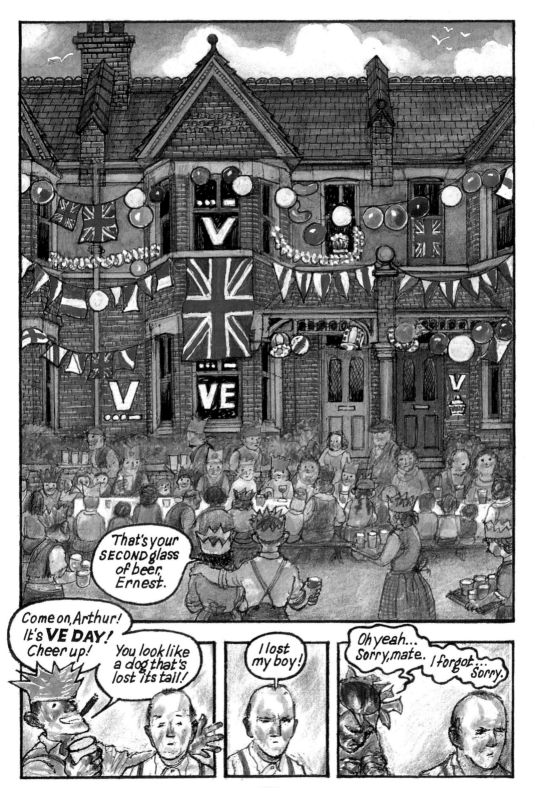

58

65

1950
~
1960

Dad... Hullo.

Dad...
When you come
home from work... Yeah?

Why don't you wash
in the BATHROOM? Blimey son! Not likely! I'm filthy, look.

Yes, I know but that is
what the bathroom is FOR! No. Not in the BATHROOM.
Not in THIS state.

But this is the KITCHEN!
All the FOOD is in HERE!
Mum is trying to COOK! No. I couldn't, son.
Not in the BATHROOM.

That laundrette is a Godsend!
I did the whole blessed lot
for two and nine.
AND it's all bone DRY!

We could chuck out the mangle and the copper.
I could get an electric thermostat for the tank!
Hot water in the SUMMER time!
MODERN!

69

73

Ooh, dear...

What shall I do if it rings when you're out?

Well, ANSWER IT! you daft ha'porth!

I don't think I like it.

Ooh! It's just like the pictures!

Yes! We might get VICTOR McLAGLEN!

He's dead.

They could still put him on.

I prefer Tyrone Power. He's more modern.

Dear, oh dear... "BRITISH RAIL LOSES SIXTEEN MILLION QUID"

It's Nationalised, isn't it?

'COURSE IT IS!

I thought so.

It says they're wanting to legalise Homo-Sexuality.   Oh? What's that?

Well...you know...it's like two BLOKES.
Only...instead of with a WOMAN, sort of with-one another...like...

I don't know what you're rambling on about, Ernest, and I don't think you do either.

I'll...er-put the kettle on, shall I, duck?
Nice cup of tea?

75

76

We should have this HI-FI now, duck.   Oh? What's that?

Well, it's sort of like having two
wirelesses on at once. One for each ear.   Extravagant.

It's a radiogram as well, though.
Plays records.   We haven't got any records.

No, but if we had, you could put them on
and hear the STEREO.   The what?

The STEREO. It comes out in STEREO.   What does?

The music from the HI-FI.
It's "PAN-OR-AM-IC SOUND" it says. 3D.   Three dee?

Yeah, 3D, 'course.   I don't think I want to bother with it.

Here! This soppy bishop says:
"Mothers who work full-time
are the enemies of family life."

It's all right for **HIM**,
living in a **PALACE**
with **SERVANTS!**

He was brought up to
different standards, Ernest.
He's a GENTLEMAN Christian.

Here Et, listen. It says we've got to be **HIP**.

What?

GROOVY, babe. And **REAL COOL**.

Just talk sense, Ernest.

We've got to **HANG LOOSE** with the **CATS**.

Cats?

YEAH, MAN!

Ernest! Go to bed.
You're overtired.
I'll make the cocoa.

You're a **SQUARE**, baby.

Oh, Ernest...
When will you grow up?

1960
~
1970

That green car! / Well? / Triumph Herald! / What about it? / Wasn't there yesterday. / There's always different cars stuck outside our house nowadays.

That one's special. / What's special about it?

It's OURS!

Oh don't be daft, Ernest.

Come on, dear. Get in. / Ooh-er... / I don't like to... / I've still got my pinny on.

I haven't done my hair.

Is it really yours?

I didn't know you could drive a proper car.

OURS, darling.

82

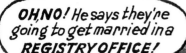

OH, NO! He says they're going to get married in a **REGISTRY OFFICE!**

Well, that's the modern way, Et.

Horrible!

Yes, but neither of them is religious.

I don't want him to be **RELIGIOUS!**

I just want him to get married in a **CHURCH!**

It's so much... nicer...

When are you going to start a family, dear?

Well... don't know really, Mum. Probably not at all.

Goodness me! Why ever not? I want to be a granny.

Well, Jean's got problems, Mum. Brain trouble.

BRAIN TROUBLE!

Yeah... well... that's just what I call it - as a sort of... joke...
She goes in and out of the loony bin.

You mean... she's - mental?

Yeah. That's one word for it. The other word is - Schizophrenia.

Oh, dear! Poor thing!

So I won't be a granny after all?

Never mind, Mum.

MAN ON THE MOON, Eh!

FANTASTIC, eh?

Oh?

What's he doing there?

Well, just walking about a bit.

Then what?

Well...come back, I suppose...

Perhaps they'll have a picnic.
That would be nice.

I think the tea would blow away
when it came out of the thermos.

Why? Is it windy up there?

No, it's gravity, dear.

Oh, I see.

Look! He's going to pick up
some pebbles...to take home.

Just like kiddies at the seaside.
Turn it off, will you?

1970 ~ 1971

Decimal Currency starts next week!   Oh yes, I've heard about it on the television.

It's dead simple! See - a bob equals **FIVE** New Pence. Two bob is **TEN** New Pence.   What's a ha'penny?

There isn't one - oh yes, there is! Half a New Pence - looks like a farthing.   What about threepenny bits?

Gone, duck. A tanner is two and a half New Pence.   And what about half a crown?

Er... well... that'll be - two bob equals ten New Pence, a tanner equals two and a half New Pence, so ten plus two and a half is... twelve and a half New Pence. Easy!   What's a penny?

An **OLD** penny... well... a shilling is five New Pence, so twelve old pennies equals five **NEW** Pence, so **ONE** old penny is... twelve into five— Um...   How many shillings are there in the pound now?

Did you have a good journey, dear?

Oh yes, OK Mum. Fine, fine.

Much traffic on the road?

Well, the A23 was a bit choked up, but after Sutton it sort of thinned out a bit...and... it got better...less traffic...um...

Here's a comb, dear.
Thanks, Mum.

Remember we used to bring the pram up here?

It's me in the pram, now.
They used to do nice teas in the balcony before the war.
Waitresses in aprons and caps...

We never did go, did we, dear?

Yes.
It was lovely.

The yobboes smashed all the windows.

That's your Labour Party for you.

95

96

In Memory of
ETHEL BRIGGS
1895-1971
ERNEST BRIGGS
1900-1971